REVELATION

SCRIPTURE NOTEBOOK

Eternal King, Everlasting Kingdom

CSB CHRISTIAN STANDARD BIBLE®
HOLMAN® BIBLES

CSB Text Edition: 2020

The interior of the CSB Scripture Notebooks were typeset using Bible Serif created by 2K/DENMARK, Højbjerg, Denmark.

Pine Leaf 979-8-3845-0968-4

Printed in China
2 3 4 5 —27 26 25 24
RRD

REVELATION

Prologue

1 The revelation of Jesus Christ that God gave him to show his
servants what must soon take place. He made it known by
sending his angel to his servant John, 2 who testified to the word
of God and to the testimony of Jesus Christ, whatever he saw.
3 Blessed is the one who reads aloud the words of this prophecy,
and blessed are those who hear the words of this prophecy and
keep what is written in it, because the time is near.

4 John: To the seven churches in Asia. Grace and peace to you
from the one who is, who was, and who is to come, and from
the seven spirits before his throne, 5 and from Jesus Christ, the
faithful witness, the firstborn from the dead and the ruler of
the kings of the earth.

To him who loves us and has set us free from our sins by his
blood, 6 and made us a kingdom, priests to his God and Father
—to him be glory and dominion forever and ever. Amen.

7 **Look, he is coming with the clouds,**
and **every eye will see him,**
even those who pierced him.
And all the tribes of the earth
will mourn over him.
So it is to be. Amen.

8 "I am the Alpha and the Omega," says the Lord God, "the one
who is, who was, and who is to come, the Almighty."

God gave revelation to Jesus via angel

Blessing to reader + hearer + keeps what is written.

Grace + peace

7 spirits - Holy Spirit manifests in 7 distinct ways ① Life John 3:5 (born of H_2O + spirit)
+ wisdom Eph 1:16-18
truth John 14:16+17 - to be gift from Jesus for believers
2 Burning Luke 3:16
holiness Romans 1:4 - God declared Jesus his son
power Acts 1:5-8 baptism of HS
3 love - Romans 15:30 Holy spirit leads Christians to pray

1 when the eyes of our understanding is enlightened - we see hope of his calling on our lives and His glory

2 Jesus will baptize us c̄ HS + fire - separate wheat from chaff (burn)

3 Paul implores the Church to strive together in prayer, embodying the love that the holy S. instills in believers.

John's Vision of the Risen Lord

9 I, John, your brother and partner in the affliction, kingdom,
and endurance that are in Jesus, was on the island called Pat-
mos because of the word of God and the testimony of Jesus.
10 I was in the Spirit on the Lord's day, and I heard a loud voice
behind me like a trumpet 11 saying, "Write on a scroll what you
see and send it to the seven churches: Ephesus, Smyrna, Perga-
mum, Thyatira, Sardis, Philadelphia, and Laodicea."

12 Then I turned to see whose voice it was that spoke to me.
When I turned I saw seven golden lampstands, 13 and among the
lampstands was one like the Son of Man, dressed in a robe and
with a golden sash wrapped around his chest. 14 The hair of his
head was white as wool — white as snow — and his eyes like a fi-
ery flame. 15 His feet were like fine bronze as it is fired in a furnace,
and his voice like the sound of cascading waters. 16 He had seven
stars in his right hand; a sharp double-edged sword came from
his mouth, and his face was shining like the sun at full strength.

17 When I saw him, I fell at his feet like a dead man. He laid his right
hand on me and said, "Don't be afraid. I am the First and the Last,
18 and the Living One. I was dead, but look — I am alive forever and
ever, and I hold the keys of death and Hades. 19 Therefore write what
you have seen, what is, and what will take place after this. 20 The
mystery of the seven stars you saw in my right hand and of the sev-
en golden lampstands is this: The seven stars are the angels of the
seven churches, and the seven lampstands are the seven churches.

9- John - your brother + companion in the
suffering + kingdom + patient endurance
that are ours in Jesus

Robe c golden sash around his chest

Feet burnished bronze - indicative of
the fact that He is the suffering servant

Vs 13-16 my favorite pic of Jesus

The Letters to the Seven Churches

The Letter to Ephesus

2 "Write to the angel of the church in Ephesus: Thus says
the one who holds the seven stars in his right hand and
who walks among the seven golden lampstands: 2 I know your
works, your labor, and your endurance, and that you cannot
tolerate evil people. You have tested those who call themselves
apostles and are not, and you have found them to be liars. 3 I
know that you have persevered and endured hardships for the
sake of my name, and you have not grown weary. 4 But I have
this against you: You have abandoned the love you had at first.
5 Remember then how far you have fallen; repent, and do the
works you did at first. Otherwise, I will come to you and re-
move your lampstand from its place, unless you repent. 6 Yet
you do have this: You hate the practices of the Nicolaitans,
which I also hate.

7 "Let anyone who has ears to hear listen to what the Spirit
says to the churches. To the one who conquers, I will give the
right to eat from the tree of life, which is in the paradise of God.

The Letter to Smyrna

8 "Write to the angel of the church in Smyrna: Thus says the
First and the Last, the one who was dead and came to life: 9 I
know your affliction and poverty, but you are rich. I know the

slander of those who say they are Jews and are not, but are a
synagogue of Satan. 10 Don't be afraid of what you are about to
suffer. Look, the devil is about to throw some of you into pris-
on to test you, and you will experience affliction for ten days.
Be faithful to the point of death, and I will give you the crown
of life.

11 "Let anyone who has ears to hear listen to what the Spir-
it says to the churches. The one who conquers will never be
harmed by the second death.

The Letter to Pergamum

12 "Write to the angel of the church in Pergamum: Thus says the
one who has the sharp, double-edged sword: 13 I know where
you live—where Satan's throne is. Yet you are holding on to
my name and did not deny your faith in me, even in the days
of Antipas, my faithful witness who was put to death among
you, where Satan lives. 14 But I have a few things against you.
You have some there who hold to the teaching of Balaam, who
taught Balak to place a stumbling block in front of the Israelites:
to eat meat sacrificed to idols and to commit sexual immorali-
ty. 15 In the same way, you also have those who hold to the teach-
ing of the Nicolaitans. 16 So repent! Otherwise, I will come to you
quickly and fight against them with the sword of my mouth.

17 "Let anyone who has ears to hear listen to what the Spirit
says to the churches. To the one who conquers, I will give some

of the hidden manna. I will also give him a white stone, and on
the stone a new name is inscribed that no one knows except
the one who receives it.

The Letter to Thyatira

18 "Write to the angel of the church in Thyatira: Thus says the
Son of God, the one whose eyes are like a fiery flame and
whose feet are like fine bronze: 19 I know your works—your
love, faithfulness, service, and endurance. I know that your last
works are greater than the first. 20 But I have this against you:
You tolerate the woman Jezebel, who calls herself a prophetess
and teaches and deceives my servants to commit sexual immo-
rality and to eat meat sacrificed to idols. 21 I gave her time to
repent, but she does not want to repent of her sexual immo-
rality. 22 Look, I will throw her into a sickbed and those who
commit adultery with her into great affliction. Unless they re-
pent of her works, 23 I will strike her children dead. Then all the
churches will know that I am the one who examines minds and
hearts, and I will give to each of you according to your works.
24 I say to the rest of you in Thyatira, who do not hold this teach-
ing, who haven't known "the so-called secrets of Satan"—as
they say—I am not putting any other burden on you. 25 Only
hold on to what you have until I come. 26 The one who conquers
and who keeps my works to the end: I will give him authority
over the nations—

27 **and he will rule them**
with an iron scepter;
he will shatter them like pottery —
28 just as I have received this from my Father. I will also give him
the morning star.
29 "Let anyone who has ears to hear listen to what the Spirit
says to the churches.

The Letter to Sardis

3 "Write to the angel of the church in Sardis: Thus says the
one who has the seven spirits of God and the seven stars: I
know your works; you have a reputation for being alive, but you
are dead. 2 Be alert and strengthen what remains, which is about
to die, for I have not found your works complete before my God.
3 Remember, then, what you have received and heard; keep it,
and repent. If you are not alert, I will come like a thief, and you
have no idea at what hour I will come upon you. 4 But you have
a few people in Sardis who have not defiled their clothes, and
they will walk with me in white, because they are worthy.
5 "In the same way, the one who conquers will be dressed in
white clothes, and I will never erase his name from the book of
life but will acknowledge his name before my Father and be-
fore his angels.
6 "Let anyone who has ears to hear listen to what the Spirit
says to the churches.

The Letter to Philadelphia

7 "Write to the angel of the church in Philadelphia: Thus says the
Holy One, the true one, the one who has the key of David, who
opens and no one will close, and who closes and no one opens:
8 I know your works. Look, I have placed before you an open
door that no one can close because you have but little power;
yet you have kept my word and have not denied my name. 9 Note
this: I will make those from the synagogue of Satan, who claim
to be Jews and are not, but are lying—I will make them come
and bow down at your feet, and they will know that I have loved
you. 10 Because you have kept my command to endure, I will also
keep you from the hour of testing that is going to come on the
whole world to test those who live on the earth. 11 I am coming
soon. Hold on to what you have, so that no one takes your crown.

12 "The one who conquers I will make a pillar in the temple of
my God, and he will never go out again. I will write on him the
name of my God and the name of the city of my God—the new
Jerusalem, which comes down out of heaven from my God—
and my new name.

13 "Let anyone who has ears to hear listen to what the Spirit
says to the churches.

The Letter to Laodicea

14 "Write to the angel of the church in Laodicea: Thus says the
Amen, the faithful and true witness, the originator of God's

creation: 15 I know your works, that you are neither cold nor hot.
I wish that you were cold or hot. 16 So, because you are lukewarm,
and neither hot nor cold, I am going to vomit you out of my mouth.
17 For you say, 'I'm rich; I have become wealthy and need nothing,'
and you don't realize that you are wretched, pitiful, poor, blind,
and naked. 18 I advise you to buy from me gold refined in the fire
so that you may be rich, white clothes so that you may be dressed
and your shameful nakedness not be exposed, and ointment to
spread on your eyes so that you may see. 19 As many as I love, I re-
buke and discipline. So be zealous and repent. 20 See! I stand at the
door and knock. If anyone hears my voice and opens the door, I
will come in to him and eat with him, and he with me.

21 "To the one who conquers I will give the right to sit with me
on my throne, just as I also conquered and sat down with my
Father on his throne.

22 "Let anyone who has ears to hear listen to what the Spirit
says to the churches."

The Throne Room of Heaven

4 After this I looked, and there in heaven was an open door.
The first voice that I had heard speaking to me like a
trumpet said, "Come up here, and I will show you what must
take place after this."

2 Immediately I was in the Spirit, and there was a throne in
heaven and someone was seated on it. 3 The one seated there

had the appearance of jasper and carnelian stone. A rainbow
that had the appearance of an emerald surrounded the throne.
4 Around the throne were twenty-four thrones, and on the
thrones sat twenty-four elders dressed in white clothes, with
golden crowns on their heads.
5 Flashes of lightning and rumblings and peals of thunder
came from the throne. Seven fiery torches were burning be-
fore the throne, which are the seven spirits of God. 6 Something
like a sea of glass, similar to crystal, was also before the throne.
Four living creatures covered with eyes in front and in back were
around the throne on each side. 7 The first living creature was like a
lion; the second living creature was like an ox; the third living creature
had a face like a man; and the fourth living creature was like a flying ea-
gle. 8 Each of the four living creatures had six wings; they were covered
with eyes around and inside. Day and night they never stop, saying,

> Holy, holy, holy,
> Lord God, the Almighty,
> who was, who is, and who is to come.

9 Whenever the living creatures give glory, honor, and thanks
to the one seated on the throne, the one who lives forever and
ever, 10 the twenty-four elders fall down before the one seated
on the throne and worship the one who lives forever and ever.
They cast their crowns before the throne and say,

> 11 Our Lord and God,
> you are worthy to receive

glory and honor and power,
because you have created all things,
and by your will
they exist and were created.

The Lamb Takes the Scroll

5 Then I saw in the right hand of the one seated on the
throne a scroll with writing on both sides, sealed with
seven seals. 2 I also saw a mighty angel proclaiming with a loud
voice, "Who is worthy to open the scroll and break its seals?"
3 But no one in heaven or on earth or under the earth was able
to open the scroll or even to look in it. 4 I wept and wept because
no one was found worthy to open the scroll or even to look in
it. 5 Then one of the elders said to me, "Do not weep. Look, the
Lion from the tribe of Judah, the Root of David, has conquered
so that he is able to open the scroll and its seven seals."

6 Then I saw one like a slaughtered lamb standing in the
midst of the throne and the four living creatures and among
the elders. He had seven horns and seven eyes, which are the
seven spirits of God sent into all the earth. 7 He went and took
the scroll out of the right hand of the one seated on the throne.

The Lamb Is Worthy

8 When he took the scroll, the four living creatures and the
twenty-four elders fell down before the Lamb. Each one had

horns - strength
eyes vision

a harp and golden bowls filled with incense, which are the
prayers of the saints. 9 And they sang a new song:

You are worthy to take the scroll
and to open its seals,
because you were slaughtered,
and you purchased people
for God by your blood
from every tribe and language
and people and nation.

10 You made them a kingdom
and priests to our God,
and they will reign on the earth.

11 Then I looked and heard the voice of many angels around
the throne, and also of the living creatures and of the elders.
Their number was countless thousands, plus thousands of
thousands. 12 They said with a loud voice,

Worthy is the Lamb who
was slaughtered
to receive power and riches
and wisdom and strength
and honor and glory and blessing!

13 I heard every creature in heaven, on earth, under the earth,
on the sea, and everything in them say,

Blessing and honor and glory and power

be to the one seated on the throne,
and to the Lamb, forever and ever!

14 The four living creatures said, "Amen," and the elders fell down and worshiped.

The First Seal on the Scroll

6 Then I saw the Lamb open one of the seven seals, and I heard one of the four living creatures say with a voice like thunder, "Come!"
2 I looked, and there was a white horse. Its rider held a bow; a crown was given to him, and he went out as a conqueror in order to conquer.

The Second Seal

3 When he opened the second seal, I heard the second living creature say, "Come!"
4 Then another horse went out, a fiery red one, and its rider was allowed to take peace from the earth, so that people would slaughter one another. And a large sword was given to him.

The Third Seal

5 When he opened the third seal, I heard the third living creature say, "Come!" And I looked, and there was a black horse. Its rider held a set of scales in his hand.
6 Then I heard something like a voice among the four living creatures say, "A quart of wheat for a denarius, and three quarts of barley for a denarius, but do not harm the oil and the wine."

The Fourth Seal

7 When he opened the fourth seal, I heard the voice of the fourth liv-
ing creature say, "Come!" 8 And I looked, and there was a pale green
horse. Its rider was named Death, and Hades was following after
him. They were given authority over a fourth of the earth, to kill by
the sword, by famine, by plague, and by the wild animals of the earth.

The Fifth Seal

9 When he opened the fifth seal, I saw under the altar the souls
of those who had been slaughtered because of the word of God
and the testimony they had given. 10 They cried out with a loud
voice, "Lord, the one who is holy and true, how long until you
judge those who live on the earth and avenge our blood?" 11 So
they were each given a white robe, and they were told to rest
a little while longer until the number would be completed of
their fellow servants and their brothers and sisters, who were
going to be killed just as they had been.

The Sixth Seal

12 Then I saw him open the sixth seal. A violent earthquake oc-
curred; the sun turned black like sackcloth made of hair; the
entire moon became like blood; 13 the stars of heaven fell to the
earth as a fig tree drops its unripe figs when shaken by a high
wind; 14 the sky was split apart like a scroll being rolled up; and
every mountain and island was moved from its place.

15 Then the kings of the earth, the nobles, the generals, the
rich, the powerful, and every slave and free person hid in the
caves and among the rocks of the mountains. 16 And they said
to the mountains and to the rocks, "Fall on us and hide us from
the face of the one seated on the throne and from the wrath of
the Lamb, 17 because the great day of their wrath has come! And
who is able to stand?"

The Sealed of Israel

7 After this I saw four angels standing at the four corners of
the earth, restraining the four winds of the earth so that
no wind could blow on the earth or on the sea or on any tree.
2 Then I saw another angel rising up from the east, who had
the seal of the living God. He cried out in a loud voice to the
four angels who were allowed to harm the earth and the sea,
3 "Don't harm the earth or the sea or the trees until we seal the
servants of our God on their foreheads." 4 And I heard the num-
ber of the sealed:

144,000 sealed from every tribe of the Israelites:
5 12,000 sealed from the tribe of Judah,
12,000 from the tribe of Reuben,
12,000 from the tribe of Gad,
6 12,000 from the tribe of Asher,
12,000 from the tribe of Naphtali,
12,000 from the tribe of Manasseh,

7 12,000 from the tribe of Simeon,
12,000 from the tribe of Levi,
12,000 from the tribe of Issachar,
8 12,000 from the tribe of Zebulun,
12,000 from the tribe of Joseph,
12,000 sealed from the tribe of Benjamin.

A Multitude from the Great Tribulation

9 After this I looked, and there was a vast multitude from ev-
ery nation, tribe, people, and language, which no one could
number, standing before the throne and before the Lamb. They
were clothed in white robes with palm branches in their hands.
10 And they cried out in a loud voice:

Salvation belongs to our God,
who is seated on the throne,
and to the Lamb!

11 All the angels stood around the throne, and along with the el-
ders and the four living creatures they fell facedown before the
throne and worshiped God, 12 saying,

Amen! Blessing and glory and wisdom
and thanksgiving and honor
and power and strength
be to our God forever and ever. Amen.

13 Then one of the elders asked me, "Who are these people in
white robes, and where did they come from?"

14 I said to him, "Sir, you know."

Then he told me: These are the ones coming out of the great tribulation. They washed their robes and made them white in the blood of the Lamb.

15 For this reason they are before the throne of God,
and they serve him day and night in his temple.
The one seated on the throne will shelter them:
16 They will no longer hunger;
they will no longer thirst;
the sun will no longer strike them,
nor will any scorching heat.
17 For the Lamb who is at the center of the throne
will shepherd them;
he will guide them to springs of the waters of life,
and God will wipe away every tear
from their eyes.

The Seventh Seal

8 When he opened the seventh seal, there was silence in
heaven for about half an hour. 2 Then I saw the seven an-
gels who stand in the presence of God; seven trumpets were
given to them. 3 Another angel, with a golden incense burner,
came and stood at the altar. He was given a large amount of in-
cense to offer with the prayers of all the saints on the golden
altar in front of the throne. 4 The smoke of the incense, with the

prayers of the saints, went up in the presence of God from the
angel's hand. 5 The angel took the incense burner, filled it with
fire from the altar, and hurled it to the earth; there were peals
of thunder, rumblings, flashes of lightning, and an earthquake.

The Seven Trumpets

6 And the seven angels who had the seven trumpets prepared
to blow them.

The First Trumpet

7 The first angel blew his trumpet, and hail and fire, mixed
with blood, were hurled to the earth. So a third of the earth
was burned up, a third of the trees were burned up, and all the
green grass was burned up.

The Second Trumpet

8 The second angel blew his trumpet, and something like a great
mountain ablaze with fire was hurled into the sea. So a third of
the sea became blood, 9 a third of the living creatures in the sea
died, and a third of the ships were destroyed.

The Third Trumpet

10 The third angel blew his trumpet, and a great star, blazing
like a torch, fell from heaven. It fell on a third of the rivers and
springs of water. 11 The name of the star is Wormwood, and a

third of the waters became wormwood. So, many of the people
died from the waters, because they had been made bitter.

The Fourth Trumpet

12 The fourth angel blew his trumpet, and a third of the sun was
struck, a third of the moon, and a third of the stars, so that a
third of them were darkened. A third of the day was without
light and also a third of the night.
13 I looked and heard an eagle flying high overhead, crying
out in a loud voice, "Woe! Woe! Woe to those who live on the
earth, because of the remaining trumpet blasts that the three
angels are about to sound!"

The Fifth Trumpet

9 The fifth angel blew his trumpet, and I saw a star that had
fallen from heaven to earth. The key for the shaft to the
abyss was given to him. 2 He opened the shaft to the abyss, and
smoke came up out of the shaft like smoke from a great fur-
nace so that the sun and the air were darkened by the smoke
from the shaft. 3 Then locusts came out of the smoke on to the
earth, and power was given to them like the power that scor-
pions have on the earth. 4 They were told not to harm the grass
of the earth, or any green plant, or any tree, but only those peo-
ple who do not have God's seal on their foreheads. 5 They were
not permitted to kill them but were to torment them for five

months; their torment is like the torment caused by a scorpion
when it stings someone. 6 In those days people will seek death
and will not find it; they will long to die, but death will flee from
them.

7 The appearance of the locusts was like horses prepared
for battle. Something like golden crowns was on their heads;
their faces were like human faces; 8 they had hair like women's
hair; their teeth were like lions' teeth; 9 they had chests like iron
breastplates; the sound of their wings was like the sound of
many chariots with horses rushing into battle; 10 and they had
tails with stingers like scorpions, so that with their tails they
had the power to harm people for five months. 11 They had as
their king the angel of the abyss; his name in Hebrew is Abad-
don, and in Greek he has the name Apollyon.

12 The first woe has passed. There are still two more woes to
come after this.

The Sixth Trumpet

13 The sixth angel blew his trumpet. From the four horns of the
golden altar that is before God, I heard a voice 14 say to the sixth
angel who had the trumpet, "Release the four angels bound at
the great river Euphrates." 15 So the four angels who were pre-
pared for the hour, day, month, and year were released to kill
a third of the human race. 16 The number of mounted troops
was two hundred million; I heard their number. 17 This is how I

saw the horses and their riders in the vision: They had breast-
plates that were fiery red, hyacinth blue, and sulfur yellow. The
heads of the horses were like the heads of lions, and from their
mouths came fire, smoke, and sulfur. 18 A third of the human
race was killed by these three plagues — by the fire, the smoke,
and the sulfur that came from their mouths. 19 For the power of
the horses is in their mouths and in their tails, because their
tails, which resemble snakes, have heads that inflict injury.

20 The rest of the people, who were not killed by these
plagues, did not repent of the works of their hands to stop wor-
shiping demons and idols of gold, silver, bronze, stone, and
wood, which cannot see, hear, or walk. 21 And they did not re-
pent of their murders, their sorceries, their sexual immorality,
or their thefts.

The Mighty Angel and the Small Scroll

10 Then I saw another mighty angel coming down from
heaven, wrapped in a cloud, with a rainbow over his
head. His face was like the sun, his legs were like pillars of fire,
2 and he held a little scroll opened in his hand. He put his right
foot on the sea, his left on the land, 3 and he called out with a loud
voice like a roaring lion. When he cried out, the seven thunders
raised their voices. 4 And when the seven thunders spoke, I was
about to write, but I heard a voice from heaven, saying, "Seal up
what the seven thunders said, and do not write it down!"

5 Then the angel that I had seen standing on the sea and on
the land raised his right hand to heaven. 6 He swore by the one
who lives forever and ever, who created heaven and what is
in it, the earth and what is in it, and the sea and what is in it,
"There will no longer be a delay, 7 but in the days when the sev-
enth angel will blow his trumpet, then the mystery of God will
be completed, as he announced to his servants the prophets."

8 Then the voice that I heard from heaven spoke to me again
and said, "Go, take the scroll that lies open in the hand of the
angel who is standing on the sea and on the land."

9 So I went to the angel and asked him to give me the little
scroll. He said to me, "Take and eat it; it will be bitter in your
stomach, but it will be as sweet as honey in your mouth."

10 Then I took the little scroll from the angel's hand and ate
it. It was as sweet as honey in my mouth, but when I ate it, my
stomach became bitter. 11 And they said to me, "You must proph-
esy again about many peoples, nations, languages, and kings."

The Two Witnesses

11 Then I was given a measuring reed like a rod, with these
words: "Go and measure the temple of God and the altar,
and count those who worship there. 2 But exclude the courtyard
outside the temple. Don't measure it, because it is given to the na-
tions, and they will trample the holy city for forty-two months.
3 I will grant my two witnesses authority to prophesy for 1,260

days, dressed in sackcloth." 4 These are the two olive trees and
the two lampstands that stand before the Lord of the earth. 5 If
anyone wants to harm them, fire comes from their mouths and
consumes their enemies; if anyone wants to harm them, he must
be killed in this way. 6 They have authority to close up the sky so
that it does not rain during the days of their prophecy. They also
have power over the waters to turn them into blood and to strike
the earth with every plague whenever they want.

The Witnesses Martyred

7 When they finish their testimony, the beast that comes up out
of the abyss will make war on them, conquer them, and kill
them. 8 Their dead bodies will lie in the main street of the great
city, which figuratively is called Sodom and Egypt, where also
their Lord was crucified. 9 And some of the peoples, tribes, lan-
guages, and nations will view their bodies for three and a half
days and not permit their bodies to be put into a tomb. 10 Those
who live on the earth will gloat over them and celebrate and
send gifts to one another because these two prophets had tor-
mented those who live on the earth.

The Witnesses Resurrected

11 But after three and a half days, the breath of life from God en-
tered them, and they stood on their feet. Great fear fell on those
who saw them. 12 Then they heard a loud voice from heaven

saying to them, "Come up here." They went up to heaven in a
cloud, while their enemies watched them. 13 At that moment a
violent earthquake took place, a tenth of the city fell, and seven
thousand people were killed in the earthquake. The survivors
were terrified and gave glory to the God of heaven.

14 The second woe has passed. Take note: The third woe is coming soon!

The Seventh Trumpet

15 The seventh angel blew his trumpet, and there were loud voices in heaven saying,

The kingdom of the world has become the kingdom
of our Lord and of his Christ,
and he will reign forever and ever.

16 The twenty-four elders, who were seated before God on their
thrones, fell facedown and worshiped God, 17 saying,

We give you thanks, Lord God, the Almighty,
who is and who was,
because you have taken your great power
and have begun to reign.
18 The nations were angry,
but your wrath has come.
The time has come
for the dead to be judged
and to give the reward

to your servants the prophets,
to the saints, and to those who fear your name,
both small and great,
and the time has come to destroy
those who destroy the earth.

19 Then the temple of God in heaven was opened, and the ark of his
covenant appeared in his temple. There were flashes of lightning,
rumblings and peals of thunder, an earthquake, and severe hail.

The Woman, the Child, and the Dragon

12 A great sign appeared in heaven: a woman clothed with
the sun, with the moon under her feet and a crown of
twelve stars on her head. 2 She was pregnant and cried out in
labor and agony as she was about to give birth. 3 Then anoth-
er sign appeared in heaven: There was a great fiery red dragon
having seven heads and ten horns, and on its heads were sev-
en crowns. 4 Its tail swept away a third of the stars in heaven
and hurled them to the earth. And the dragon stood in front of
the woman who was about to give birth, so that when she did
give birth it might devour her child. 5 She gave birth to a Son, a
male who is going to rule all nations with an iron rod. Her child
was caught up to God and to his throne. 6 The woman fled into
the wilderness, where she had a place prepared by God, to be
nourished there for 1,260 days.

The Dragon Thrown Out of Heaven

7 Then war broke out in heaven: Michael and his angels fought
against the dragon. The dragon and his angels also fought, 8 but
he could not prevail, and there was no place for them in heav-
en any longer. 9 So the great dragon was thrown out — the an-
cient serpent, who is called the devil and Satan, the one who
deceives the whole world. He was thrown to earth, and his an-
gels with him. 10 Then I heard a loud voice in heaven say,

The salvation and the power
and the kingdom of our God
and the authority of his Christ
have now come,
because the accuser of our brothers and sisters,
who accuses them
before our God day and night,
has been thrown down.

11 They conquered him
by the blood of the Lamb
and by the word of their testimony;
for they did not love their lives
to the point of death.

12 Therefore rejoice, you heavens,
and you who dwell in them!
Woe to the earth and the sea,
because the devil has come down to you

with great fury,
because he knows his time is short.

The Woman Persecuted

13 When the dragon saw that he had been thrown down to the
earth, he persecuted the woman who had given birth to the
male child. 14 The woman was given two wings of a great eagle,
so that she could fly from the serpent's presence to her place in
the wilderness, where she was nourished for a time, times, and
half a time. 15 From his mouth the serpent spewed water like a
river flowing after the woman, to sweep her away with a flood.
16 But the earth helped the woman. The earth opened its mouth
and swallowed up the river that the dragon had spewed from
his mouth. 17 So the dragon was furious with the woman and
went off to wage war against the rest of her offspring — those
who keep the commands of God and hold firmly to the testi-
mony about Jesus.

The Beast from the Sea

18 The dragon stood on the sand of the sea.

13 And I saw a beast coming up out of the sea. It had ten
horns and seven heads. On its horns were ten crowns,
and on its heads were blasphemous names. 2 The beast I saw
was like a leopard, its feet were like a bear's, and its mouth was
like a lion's mouth. The dragon gave the beast his power, his

throne, and great authority. [3] One of its heads appeared to be
fatally wounded, but its fatal wound was healed.

The whole earth was amazed and followed the beast. [4] They
worshiped the dragon because he gave authority to the beast.
And they worshiped the beast, saying, "Who is like the beast?
Who is able to wage war against it?"

[5] The beast was given a mouth to utter boasts and blasphe-
mies. It was allowed to exercise authority for forty-two months.
[6] It began to speak blasphemies against God: to blaspheme his
name and his dwelling—those who dwell in heaven. [7] And it
was permitted to wage war against the saints and to conquer
them. It was also given authority over every tribe, people, lan-
guage, and nation. [8] All those who live on the earth will worship
it, everyone whose name was not written from the foundation
of the world in the book of life of the Lamb who was slaughtered.

[9] If anyone has ears to hear, let him listen.

10 If anyone is to be taken captive,
into captivity he goes.
If anyone is to be killed with a sword,
with a sword he will be killed.

This calls for endurance and faithfulness from the saints.

The Beast from the Earth

[11] Then I saw another beast coming up out of the earth; it had
two horns like a lamb, but it spoke like a dragon. [12] It exercises

all the authority of the first beast on its behalf and compels
the earth and those who live on it to worship the first beast,
whose fatal wound was healed. 13 It also performs great signs,
even causing fire to come down from heaven to earth in front
of people. 14 It deceives those who live on the earth because of
the signs that it is permitted to perform in the presence of the
beast, telling those who live on the earth to make an image of
the beast who was wounded by the sword and yet lived. 15 It was
permitted to give breath to the image of the beast, so that the
image of the beast could both speak and cause whoever would
not worship the image of the beast to be killed. 16 And it makes
everyone — small and great, rich and poor, free and slave — to
receive a mark on his right hand or on his forehead, 17 so that
no one can buy or sell unless he has the mark: the beast's name
or the number of its name.

18 This calls for wisdom: Let the one who has understanding
calculate the number of the beast, because it is the number of a
person. Its number is 666.

The Lamb and the 144,000

14 Then I looked, and there was the Lamb, standing on
Mount Zion, and with him were 144,000 who had his
name and his Father's name written on their foreheads. 2 I
heard a sound from heaven like the sound of cascading waters
and like the rumbling of loud thunder. The sound I heard was

like harpists playing on their harps. 3 They sang a new song be-
fore the throne and before the four living creatures and the el-
ders, but no one could learn the song except the 144,000 who
had been redeemed from the earth. 4 These are the ones who
have not defiled themselves with women, since they remained
virgins. These are the ones who follow the Lamb wherever he
goes. They were redeemed from humanity as the firstfruits for
God and the Lamb. 5 No lie was found in their mouths; they are
blameless.

The Proclamation of Three Angels

6 Then I saw another angel flying high overhead, with the eter-
nal gospel to announce to the inhabitants of the earth — to ev-
ery nation, tribe, language, and people. 7 He spoke with a loud
voice: "Fear God and give him glory, because the hour of his
judgment has come. Worship the one who made heaven and
earth, the sea and the springs of water."

8 And another, a second angel, followed, saying, "It has fallen,
Babylon the Great has fallen. She made all the nations drink the
wine of her sexual immorality, which brings wrath."

9 And another, a third angel, followed them and spoke with
a loud voice: "If anyone worships the beast and its image and
receives a mark on his forehead or on his hand, 10 he will also
drink the wine of God's wrath, which is poured full strength
into the cup of his anger. He will be tormented with fire and

sulfur in the sight of the holy angels and in the sight of the
Lamb, 11 and the smoke of their torment will go up forever
and ever. There is no rest day or night for those who worship
the beast and its image, or anyone who receives the mark of
its name. 12 This calls for endurance from the saints, who keep
God's commands and their faith in Jesus."

13 Then I heard a voice from heaven saying, "Write: Blessed
are the dead who die in the Lord from now on."

"Yes," says the Spirit, "so they will rest from their labors, since their works follow them."

Reaping the Earth's Harvest

14 Then I looked, and there was a white cloud, and one like the
Son of Man was seated on the cloud, with a golden crown on
his head and a sharp sickle in his hand. 15 Another angel came
out of the temple, crying out in a loud voice to the one who was
seated on the cloud, "Use your sickle and reap, for the time to
reap has come, since the harvest of the earth is ripe." 16 So the
one seated on the cloud swung his sickle over the earth, and
the earth was harvested.

17 Then another angel who also had a sharp sickle came out of
the temple in heaven. 18 Yet another angel, who had authority over
fire, came from the altar, and he called with a loud voice to the
one who had the sharp sickle, "Use your sharp sickle and gather
the clusters of grapes from the vineyard of the earth, because its

grapes have ripened." 19 So the angel swung his sickle at the earth
and gathered the grapes from the vineyard of the earth, and he
threw them into the great winepress of God's wrath. 20 Then the
press was trampled outside the city, and blood flowed out of the
press up to the horses' bridles for about 180 miles.

Preparation for the Bowl Judgments

15 Then I saw another great and awe-inspiring sign in heav-
en: seven angels with the seven last plagues; for with
them God's wrath will be completed. 2 I also saw something like
a sea of glass mixed with fire, and those who had won the vic-
tory over the beast, its image, and the number of its name, were
standing on the sea of glass with harps from God. 3 They sang
the song of God's servant Moses and the song of the Lamb:

Great and awe-inspiring are your works,
Lord God, the Almighty;
just and true are your ways,
King of the nations.
4 Lord, who will not fear
and glorify your name?
For you alone are holy.
All the nations will come
and worship before you
because your righteous acts
have been revealed.

5 After this I looked, and the heavenly temple — the taberna-
cle of testimony — was opened. 6 Out of the temple came the
seven angels with the seven plagues, dressed in pure, bright
linen, with golden sashes wrapped around their chests. 7 One
of the four living creatures gave the seven angels seven golden
bowls filled with the wrath of God who lives forever and ever.
8 Then the temple was filled with smoke from the glory of God
and from his power, and no one could enter the temple until
the seven plagues of the seven angels were completed.

The First Bowl

16 Then I heard a loud voice from the temple saying to the
seven angels, "Go and pour out the seven bowls of God's
wrath on the earth." 2 The first went and poured out his bowl on
the earth, and severely painful sores broke out on the people
who had the mark of the beast and who worshiped its image.

The Second Bowl

3 The second poured out his bowl into the sea. It turned to blood
like that of a dead person, and all life in the sea died.

The Third Bowl

4 The third poured out his bowl into the rivers and the springs
of water, and they became blood. 5 I heard the angel of the wa-
ters say,

You are just,
the Holy One, who is and who was,
because you have passed judgment
on these things.

6 Because they poured out
the blood of the saints and the prophets,
you have given them blood to drink;
they deserve it!

7 I heard the altar say,

Yes, Lord God, the Almighty,
true and just are your judgments.

The Fourth Bowl

8 The fourth poured out his bowl on the sun. It was allowed to
scorch people with fire, 9 and people were scorched by the in-
tense heat. So they blasphemed the name of God, who has the power over these plagues, and they did not repent and give him glory.

The Fifth Bowl

10 The fifth poured out his bowl on the throne of the beast, and its kingdom was plunged into darkness. People gnawed their
tongues because of their pain 11 and blasphemed the God of
heaven because of their pains and their sores, but they did not repent of their works.

The Sixth Bowl

12 The sixth poured out his bowl on the great river Euphrates, and its
water was dried up to prepare the way for the kings from the east.
13 Then I saw three unclean spirits like frogs coming from the drag-
on's mouth, from the beast's mouth, and from the mouth of the
false prophet. 14 For they are demonic spirits performing signs, who
travel to the kings of the whole world to assemble them for the bat-
tle on the great day of God, the Almighty. 15 "Look, I am coming like a
thief. Blessed is the one who is alert and remains clothed so that he
may not go around naked and people see his shame." 16 So they as-
sembled the kings at the place called in Hebrew, Armageddon.

The Seventh Bowl

17 Then the seventh poured out his bowl into the air, and a loud
voice came out of the temple from the throne, saying, "It is
done!" 18 There were flashes of lightning, rumblings, and peals
of thunder. And a severe earthquake occurred like no other
since people have been on the earth, so great was the quake.
19 The great city split into three parts, and the cities of the na-
tions fell. Babylon the Great was remembered in God's pres-
ence; he gave her the cup filled with the wine of his fierce anger.
20 Every island fled, and the mountains disappeared. 21 Enor-
mous hailstones, each weighing about a hundred pounds,
fell from the sky on people, and they blasphemed God for the
plague of hail because that plague was extremely severe.

The Woman and the Scarlet Beast

17 Then one of the seven angels who had the seven bowls came and spoke with me: "Come, I will show you the judgment of the notorious prostitute who is seated on many waters. 2 The kings of the earth committed sexual immorality with her, and those who live on the earth became drunk on the wine of her sexual immorality." 3 Then he carried me away in the Spirit to a wilderness.

I saw a woman sitting on a scarlet beast that was covered with blasphemous names and had seven heads and ten horns. 4 The woman was dressed in purple and scarlet, adorned with gold, jewels, and pearls. She had a golden cup in her hand filled with everything detestable and with the impurities of her prostitution. 5 On her forehead was written a name, a mystery: BABYLON THE GREAT, THE MOTHER OF PROSTITUTES AND OF THE DETESTABLE THINGS OF THE EARTH. 6 Then I saw that the woman was drunk with the blood of the saints and with the blood of the witnesses to Jesus. When I saw her, I was greatly astonished.

The Meaning of the Woman and of the Beast

7 Then the angel said to me, "Why are you astonished? I will explain to you the mystery of the woman and of the beast, with the seven heads and the ten horns, that carries her. 8 The beast that you saw was, and is not, and is about to come up from the abyss and go to destruction. Those who live on the earth whose

names have not been written in the book of life from the foun-
dation of the world will be astonished when they see the beast
that was, and is not, and is to come. 9 This calls for a mind that
has wisdom.

"The seven heads are seven mountains on which the wom-
an is seated. They are also seven kings: 10 Five have fallen, one
is, the other has not yet come, and when he comes, he must re-
main for only a little while. 11 The beast that was and is not, is it-
self an eighth king, but it belongs to the seven and is going to
destruction. 12 The ten horns you saw are ten kings who have
not yet received a kingdom, but they will receive authority as
kings with the beast for one hour. 13 These have one purpose,
and they give their power and authority to the beast. 14 These
will make war against the Lamb, but the Lamb will conquer
them because he is Lord of lords and King of kings. Those with
him are called, chosen, and faithful."

15 He also said to me, "The waters you saw, where the pros-
titute was seated, are peoples, multitudes, nations, and lan-
guages. 16 The ten horns you saw, and the beast, will hate the
prostitute. They will make her desolate and naked, devour her
flesh, and burn her up with fire. 17 For God has put it into their
hearts to carry out his plan by having one purpose and to give
their kingdom to the beast until the words of God are fulfilled.
18 And the woman you saw is the great city that has royal pow-
er over the kings of the earth."

The Fall of Babylon the Great

18 After this I saw another angel with great authority
coming down from heaven, and the earth was illumi-
nated by his splendor. 2 He called out in a mighty voice:

It has fallen,
Babylon the Great has fallen!
She has become a home for demons,
a haunt for every unclean spirit,
a haunt for every unclean bird,
and a haunt for every unclean and despicable beast.
3 For all the nations have drunk
the wine of her sexual immorality,
which brings wrath.
The kings of the earth
have committed sexual immorality with her,
and the merchants of the earth
have grown wealthy from her sensuality and excess.

4 Then I heard another voice from heaven:

Come out of her, my people,
so that you will not share in her sins
or receive any of her plagues.
5 For her sins are piled up to heaven,
and God has remembered her crimes.
6 Pay her back the way she also paid,
and double it according to her works.

In the cup in which she mixed,
mix a double portion for her.
7 As much as she glorified herself and indulged her sensual
and excessive ways,
give her that much torment and grief.
For she says in her heart,
"I sit as a queen;
I am not a widow,
and I will never see grief."
8 For this reason her plagues will come
in just one day —
death and grief and famine.
She will be burned up with fire,
because the Lord God who judges her
is mighty.

The World Mourns Babylon's Fall

9 The kings of the earth who have committed sexual immoral-
ity and shared her sensual and excessive ways will weep and
mourn over her when they see the smoke from her burning.
10 They will stand far off in fear of her torment, saying,

Woe, woe, the great city,
Babylon, the mighty city!
For in a single hour
your judgment has come.

[11] The merchants of the earth will weep and mourn over her, be-
cause no one buys their cargo any longer — [12] cargo of gold, sil-
ver, jewels, and pearls; fine linen, purple, silk, and scarlet; all kinds
of fragrant wood products; objects of ivory; objects of expensive
wood, brass, iron, and marble; [13] cinnamon, spice, incense, myrrh,
and frankincense; wine, olive oil, fine flour, and grain; cattle and
sheep; horses and carriages; and slaves — human lives.

14 The fruit you craved has left you.
All your splendid and glamorous things are gone;
they will never find them again.

[15] The merchants of these things, who became rich from her,
will stand far off in fear of her torment, weeping and mourn-
ing, [16] saying,

Woe, woe, the great city,
dressed in fine linen, purple, and scarlet,
adorned with gold, jewels, and pearls;
17 for in a single hour
such fabulous wealth was destroyed!

And every shipmaster, seafarer, the sailors, and all who do
business by sea, stood far off [18] as they watched the smoke from
her burning and kept crying out, "Who was like the great city?"
[19] They threw dust on their heads and kept crying out, weeping,
and mourning,

Woe, woe, the great city,
where all those who have ships on the sea
became rich from her wealth;
for in a single hour she was destroyed.
20 Rejoice over her, heaven,
and you saints, apostles, and prophets,
because God has pronounced on her the judgment she
passed on you!

The Finality of Babylon's Fall

21 Then a mighty angel picked up a stone like a large millstone
and threw it into the sea, saying,

In this way, Babylon the great city
will be thrown down violently
and never be found again.
22 The sound of harpists, musicians,
flutists, and trumpeters
will never be heard in you again;
no craftsman of any trade
will ever be found in you again;
the sound of a mill
will never be heard in you again;
23 the light of a lamp
will never shine in you again;
and the voice of a groom and bride

will never be heard in you again.
All this will happen
because your merchants
were the nobility of the earth,
because all the nations were deceived
by your sorcery.
24 In her was found the blood of prophets and saints,
and of all those slaughtered on the earth.

Celebration in Heaven

19 After this I heard something like the loud voice of a vast
multitude in heaven, saying,

Hallelujah!
Salvation, glory, and power belong to our God,
2 because his judgments are true and righteous,
because he has judged the notorious prostitute
who corrupted the earth with her sexual immorality;
and he has avenged the blood of his servants
that was on her hands.

3 A second time they said,

Hallelujah!
Her smoke ascends forever and ever!

4 Then the twenty-four elders and the four living creatures fell
down and worshiped God, who is seated on the throne, saying,

Amen! Hallelujah!

5 A voice came from the throne, saying,

Praise our God,
all his servants, and the ones who fear him,
both small and great!

6 Then I heard something like the voice of a vast multitude, like
the sound of cascading waters, and like the rumbling of loud
thunder, saying,

Hallelujah, because our Lord God, the Almighty,
reigns!
7 Let us be glad, rejoice, and give him glory,
because the marriage of the Lamb has come,
and his bride has prepared herself.
8 She was given fine linen to wear, bright and pure.

For the fine linen represents the righteous acts of the saints.

9 Then he said to me, "Write: Blessed are those invited to the
marriage feast of the Lamb!" He also said to me, "These words
of God are true." 10 Then I fell at his feet to worship him, but he
said to me, "Don't do that! I am a fellow servant with you and
your brothers and sisters who hold firmly to the testimony of
Jesus. Worship God, because the testimony of Jesus is the spir-
it of prophecy."

The Rider on a White Horse

11 Then I saw heaven opened, and there was a white horse. Its
rider is called Faithful and True, and with justice he judges and

makes war. 12 His eyes were like a fiery flame, and many crowns
were on his head. He had a name written that no one knows ex-
cept himself. 13 He wore a robe dipped in blood, and his name
is called the Word of God. 14 The armies that were in heaven
followed him on white horses, wearing pure white linen. 15 A
sharp sword came from his mouth, so that he might strike the
nations with it. He will rule them with an iron rod. He will also
trample the winepress of the fierce anger of God, the Almighty.
16 And he has a name written on his robe and on his thigh: KING
OF KINGS AND LORD OF LORDS.

The Beast and Its Armies Defeated

17 Then I saw an angel standing in the sun, and he called out in a
loud voice, saying to all the birds flying high overhead, "Come,
gather together for the great supper of God, 18 so that you may
eat the flesh of kings, the flesh of military commanders, the
flesh of the mighty, the flesh of horses and of their riders, and
the flesh of everyone, both free and slave, small and great."

19 Then I saw the beast, the kings of the earth, and their ar-
mies gathered together to wage war against the rider on the
horse and against his army. 20 But the beast was taken pris-
oner, and along with it the false prophet, who had performed
the signs in its presence. He deceived those who accepted the
mark of the beast and those who worshiped its image with
these signs. Both of them were thrown alive into the lake of fire

that burns with sulfur. 21 The rest were killed with the sword
that came from the mouth of the rider on the horse, and all the
birds ate their fill of their flesh.

Satan Bound

20 Then I saw an angel coming down from heaven hold-
ing the key to the abyss and a great chain in his hand.
2 He seized the dragon, that ancient serpent who is the dev-
il and Satan, and bound him for a thousand years. 3 He threw
him into the abyss, closed it, and put a seal on it so that he
would no longer deceive the nations until the thousand years
were completed. After that, he must be released for a short
time.

The Saints Reign with Christ

4 Then I saw thrones, and people seated on them who were giv-
en authority to judge. I also saw the souls of those who had
been beheaded because of their testimony about Jesus and be-
cause of the word of God, who had not worshiped the beast or
his image, and who had not accepted the mark on their fore-
heads or their hands. They came to life and reigned with Christ
for a thousand years. 5 The rest of the dead did not come to life
until the thousand years were completed.

This is the first resurrection. 6 Blessed and holy is the one
who shares in the first resurrection! The second death has no

power over them, but they will be priests of God and of Christ,
and they will reign with him for a thousand years.

Satanic Rebellion Crushed

7 When the thousand years are completed, Satan will be re-
leased from his prison 8 and will go out to deceive the nations
at the four corners of the earth, Gog and Magog, to gather them
for battle. Their number is like the sand of the sea. 9 They came
up across the breadth of the earth and surrounded the en-
campment of the saints, the beloved city. Then fire came down
from heaven and consumed them. 10 The devil who deceived
them was thrown into the lake of fire and sulfur where the
beast and the false prophet are, and they will be tormented day
and night forever and ever.

The Great White Throne Judgment

11 Then I saw a great white throne and one seated on it. Earth
and heaven fled from his presence, and no place was found for
them. 12 I also saw the dead, the great and the small, standing
before the throne, and books were opened. Another book was
opened, which is the book of life, and the dead were judged
according to their works by what was written in the books.
13 Then the sea gave up the dead that were in it, and death and
Hades gave up the dead that were in them; each one was judged
according to their works. 14 Death and Hades were thrown into

the lake of fire. This is the second death, the lake of fire. 15 And anyone whose name was not found written in the book of life was thrown into the lake of fire.

The New Creation

21 Then I saw a new heaven and a new earth; for the first heaven and the first earth had passed away, and the sea was no more. 2 I also saw the holy city, the new Jerusalem, coming down out of heaven from God, prepared like a bride adorned for her husband.

3 Then I heard a loud voice from the throne: Look, God's dwelling is with humanity, and he will live with them. They will be his peoples, and God himself will be with them and will be their God. 4 He will wipe away every tear from their eyes. Death will be no more; grief, crying, and pain will be no more, because the previous things have passed away.

5 Then the one seated on the throne said, "Look, I am making everything new." He also said, "Write, because these words are faithful and true." 6 Then he said to me, "It is done! I am the Alpha and the Omega, the beginning and the end. I will freely give to the thirsty from the spring of the water of life. 7 The one who conquers will inherit these things, and I will be his God, and he will be my son. 8 But the cowards, faithless, detestable, murderers, sexually immoral, sorcerers, idolaters, and all liars — their share will be in the lake that burns with fire and sulfur, which is the second death."

The New Jerusalem

9 Then one of the seven angels, who had held the seven bowls
filled with the seven last plagues, came and spoke with me:
"Come, I will show you the bride, the wife of the Lamb." 10 He
then carried me away in the Spirit to a great, high mountain
and showed me the holy city, Jerusalem, coming down out of
heaven from God, 11 arrayed with God's glory. Her radiance was
like a precious jewel, like a jasper stone, clear as crystal. 12 The
city had a massive high wall, with twelve gates. Twelve angels
were at the gates; the names of the twelve tribes of Israel's sons
were inscribed on the gates. 13 There were three gates on the
east, three gates on the north, three gates on the south, and
three gates on the west. 14 The city wall had twelve foundations,
and the twelve names of the twelve apostles of the Lamb were
on the foundations.

15 The one who spoke with me had a golden measuring rod to
measure the city, its gates, and its wall. 16 The city is laid out in
a square; its length and width are the same. He measured the
city with the rod at 12,000 *stadia*. Its length, width, and height
are equal. 17 Then he measured its wall, 144 cubits according
to human measurement, which the angel used. 18 The build-
ing material of its wall was jasper, and the city was pure gold
clear as glass. 19 The foundations of the city wall were adorned
with every kind of jewel: the first foundation is jasper, the sec-
ond sapphire, the third chalcedony, the fourth emerald, 20 the

fifth sardonyx, the sixth carnelian, the seventh chrysolite, the eighth beryl, the ninth topaz, the tenth chrysoprase, the eleventh jacinth, the twelfth amethyst. 21 The twelve gates are twelve pearls; each individual gate was made of a single pearl. The main street of the city was pure gold, transparent as glass.

22 I did not see a temple in it, because the Lord God the Almighty and the Lamb are its temple. 23 The city does not need the sun or the moon to shine on it, because the glory of God illuminates it, and its lamp is the Lamb. 24 The nations will walk by its light, and the kings of the earth will bring their glory into it. 25 Its gates will never close by day because it will never be night there. 26 They will bring the glory and honor of the nations into it. 27 Nothing unclean will ever enter it, nor anyone who does what is detestable or false, but only those written in the Lamb's book of life.

The Source of Life

22 Then he showed me the river of the water of life, clear as crystal, flowing from the throne of God and of the Lamb 2 down the middle of the city's main street. The tree of life was on each side of the river, bearing twelve kinds of fruit, producing its fruit every month. The leaves of the tree are for healing the nations, 3 and there will no longer be any curse. The throne of God and of the Lamb will be in the city, and his servants will worship him. 4 They will see his face, and his name

will be on their foreheads. 5 Night will be no more; people will
not need the light of a lamp or the light of the sun, because the
Lord God will give them light, and they will reign forever and
ever.

The Time Is Near

6 Then he said to me, "These words are faithful and true. The
Lord, the God of the spirits of the prophets, has sent his angel
to show his servants what must soon take place."

7 "Look, I am coming soon! Blessed is the one who keeps the
words of the prophecy of this book."

8 I, John, am the one who heard and saw these things. When
I heard and saw them, I fell down to worship at the feet of the
angel who had shown them to me. 9 But he said to me, "Don't do
that! I am a fellow servant with you, your brothers the proph-
ets, and those who keep the words of this book. Worship God!"

10 Then he said to me, "Don't seal up the words of the prophe-
cy of this book, because the time is near. 11 Let the unrighteous
go on in unrighteousness; let the filthy still be filthy; let the
righteous go on in righteousness; let the holy still be holy."

12 "Look, I am coming soon, and my reward is with me to re-
pay each person according to his work. 13 I am the Alpha and
the Omega, the first and the last, the beginning and the end.

14 "Blessed are those who wash their robes, so that they may
have the right to the tree of life and may enter the city by the

gates. 15 Outside are the dogs, the sorcerers, the sexually im-
moral, the murderers, the idolaters, and everyone who loves
and practices falsehood.

16 "I, Jesus, have sent my angel to attest these things to you for
the churches. I am the Root and descendant of David, the bright
morning star."

17 Both the Spirit and the bride say, "Come! " Let anyone who
hears, say, "Come! " Let the one who is thirsty come. Let the one
who desires take the water of life freely.

18 I testify to everyone who hears the words of the prophe-
cy of this book: If anyone adds to them, God will add to him
the plagues that are written in this book. 19 And if anyone takes
away from the words of the book of this prophecy, God will
take away his share of the tree of life and the holy city, which
are written about in this book.

20 He who testifies about these things says, "Yes, I am com-
ing soon."

Amen! Come, Lord Jesus!

21 The grace of the Lord Jesus be with everyone. Amen.